MARRIAGE:
AS GOD INTENDED IT TO BE

OLATOKUNBO OJO

MARRIAGE: AS GOD INTENDED IT TO BE

ISBN : 978-8-68614-619-8

Unless otherwise indicated, Bible quotations are taken from the New King James Version (NKJV) of the Holy Bible.

Published by:
Grace Springs Africa Publishers,
15, Association Avenue, Ilupeju, Lagos.
P.O. Box 698, Shomolu, Lagos, Nigeria.

Tel: 08141381090/1
info@gracespringsafrica.org
www.gracespringsafrica.org

Contents

dedication

I dedicate this book to all godly women who fear the Lord and who believe the institution of marriage originates from God.

Also to those who stood by me and comforted me in my times of trial through their prayers. God bless you.

acknowledgement

First and foremost, I want to appreciate the Almighty God for showing me why He created marriage and giving me the inspiration to write this book. There is no one like my Jehovah.

To my wonderful Parents, Late (Dr) & Mrs C.O. Majekodunmi. Thanks a million for all your support and love. Dad, I miss u dearly. Mum, God bless you mightily. I could not have had better parents.

I want to thank God for Pastor Taiwo Odukoya for teaching me to stay focused on the Word, I also thank God for directing my steps to Fountain of Life Church, where I was thought to focus on Jesus and not my challenges.

Pastor Tosin Sowemimo, Pastor Femi Megbope, and Mrs Moji Aribaloye thank you for your seasonal wisdom and words of encouragement .

I especially want to thank my husband for being a caring and loving man against all odds. Words cannot describe how much I love you. I thank God for all He has done and what he is still doing in our marriage.

prologue

The truth is, there are few institutions as endangered as marriage today. Divorce statistics are the highest they have ever been. More children are being raised by single parents than ever before, and the notion that marriage is a fragile, fickle contraption that can be collapsed at will is being reinforced in the minds of our children. A failed or failing marriage is one of the most devastating experiences anyone can go through. Its impact goes beyond the marriage itself and extends to every facet of the individual lives that make or made it up. I have been there before. I am well acquainted with the pain that attends having your marriage on the brink of collapse as well as the joy of pulling back into a place of happiness and fulfilment. And I know for sure that no marriage is too far gone to be salvaged.

Young men and young women must not be too disturbed by the alarming prevalence of divorce. Even if there is one divorce in every six marriages, think of the millions of happy homes where men and women and their children live together in loyalty and in love. A happy home is as near to heaven as we ever come in this world. The medieval knights had a saying that no knight was properly fitted for battle unless the hand of a woman had buckled his armor.

A good marriage is possible. It does not come easily, but you can have it. In fact, most great marriages go through trials. But no matter how steep your trials may be, you can be assured that with the love of God inside of you, you will surely have the wonderful marriage that God has purposed for you. I lay, unabashedly, the turnaround my marriage experienced at the feet of God. It was His grace and strength that saw me through, and it is that same grace that has inspired me to share the experiences, lessons and testimony of what the Lord has done for me, knowing that He is able and willing to do it for as many marriages out there going through tough times. For those experiencing some measure of joy in their marriage, I know God can make our experiences even better.

I remember vividly the day I decided to cease battling to make my marriage work in my own strength and cede control over to God. My husband and I travelled to South Africa in September 2012 and one night, unable to sleep, I decided to seek God's face. I picked up a book on the Holy Spirit, and began to read. I was suddenly seized by a strong urge to pray for someone and I had no idea who the person was, so I prayed in the spirit. The next night, at about the same time, I heard a voice loud and clear saying, "Women have forgotten why I created marriage so there will be plenty of divorce especially amongst Christians." So I started praying for all married women, especially those who were going through serious challenges. I prayed that God would take charge of their issues. When I woke up I just did not understand any of what was happening. The following night God spoke to me again saying, we are to be helpmates to our husbands not mothers. Then I began to ask myself "Was I being a mother to my husband or a helpmate?" So I prayed: "Lord let me be a helpmate to my husband. I leave him to you to change him." Then God told me He had an assignment for me: touch the lives of other women when you get back home by reminding them of the purpose of marriage -if not there would be plenty of divorce.

This is a big assignment," I thought to myself. "Am I ready for this, given the imperfection of my own marriage?" But I could hear God telling me my marriage would be healed through the fulfilment of the assignment and that the challenges I had been going through were preparing me to help others believe He created marriage and has a template for making it work. I just kept asking Him to give me the Grace to overcome all my challenges and to enable me be the wife He has created me to be. That day I told God, "I have handed my marriage over to you."I continued with my life like I had no problems at all. I allowed the Lord work in me to become more patient, less talkative and less aggressive. My attitude changed. My marriage began to turn around.

As my marital problems became a distant memory, God told me to write a book and gave me this title. He told me that many of His children have forgotten the reason why He created marriage. Many women go into marriage for the wrong reasons and they allow themselves to be distracted from Jesus and His precepts. God's intention is for the wife to be a helpmate and to submit to her husband (no matter what his status is) and always show him respect. That's why it is important to seek God's approval before you get married. Now I know that I have to be more careful in how I behave towards my challenges and where I am weak I ask that God should help me, and indeed He is helping me. After sixteen or seventeen years of marriage I am now beginning to fully enjoy my marriage, even though it is not perfect, but with God's help it has improved dramatically. As I have continued to live God's Word, I have seen changes in the lives of my husband and myself. If you want your marriage to work you must invest in it 100%.

As you read this book, I pray that God will touch your heart, and in any area that you are having challenges in your marriage, God will surely visit you. Do not give up on your marriage. God has a purpose for you in that marriage because it is all about Him.

1

A Marriage in Turmoil

No marriage is easy. Each one comes with its own peculiar challenge. Nkechi's did. Nkechi got married a while back. The circumstances predating their union strongly suggested God had a hand in their marriage. Unfortunately, the marriage was plagued with challenges from the outset. She knew (her husband) as an outgoing person but thought it wouldn't be a problem because God had given the go ahead. Then the late nights began. Each night she would sit up late asking God to bring her husband back in one piece. The late nights brought waves of quarrels that got increasingly heated.

The first time he hit her, she reported him to his parents. She found their response queer -"divorce." She certainly had no plan to do so, choosing instead to stick with her husband no matter what. She had underestimated how difficult this would be. Nkechi had previously made the transition from church goer to firm believer. God was her mainstay now. He would have to prove Himself. But not after she went through the crucible. Their marital problems did not abate.

She turned to the only source of succour she knew -God. Her lamentations rose to the heavens day and night. Why had God allowed her to face nothing but pain in her marriage? The problems were just too difficult. It was impossible for her to cope. She kept praying. He kept misbehaving.

One Sunday afternoon, her husband came back home from one of his late night outings and wanted to strangle her. He asked her to pack her belongings together and leave the house. "But something inside of her said she should hang in there". She ran out of the house barefoot with her child not knowing exactly where she was going. She finally decided to head for her parents' house.

When she got there she did not tell them she was planning to stay until they noticed it was getting late and asked when she would start heading home. She told them that she would not be going back home that night. The next day, unable to keep up the farce any longer, she broke down and opened up.

She remained with her parents until she was able to put herself together. She maintained communication with her husband throughout this period. She kept an eye out for changed behaviour but never saw it. Despite of no change she went back to her husband, as years went by, Nkechi could not cope with her husband behaviours, so, she gave up and went back to stay with her parents. She renewed her waning zeal for God and church activities. God spoke to her to join a department and she promptly obeyed. Frustrated by her marital ordeals, she resumed her divorce proceedings after three years of seperation.

Sceptical about her decision, she handed God a fleece: if the lawyer came up with all the needed documentation at a particular time she would go ahead. If he did not, she would take it as a sign from God and back out. He did not. She turned her back on the divorce again and fixed her attention on God. She dredged up every resource she could find hoping to find any shred of evidence that God supported a divorce. She found none.

"I kept asking myself, is this kind of life I want for myself and my child?" Nkechi recalls.

"I guess God had been speaking to me but I had not realised it. Every night I would cry heavily to God to intervene, as I was getting tired of all my martial struggles. I held on tenaciously to every word that proceeded from the pulpit. This went on for some time until one day, in the early hours of the morning, about 3am, a voice woke me up and told me to go back to my husband," She said.

She looked around but did not see anybody. So she ignored the voice and went back to sleep. She was woken up again by the same voice with the same instruction. "Go back where? To suffer? I can't, he needs to change," she loudly replied. But the voice persisted: "Go back to your husband. Seek ye first the kingdom of God and everything will be added onto you (Matthew 6:33)."

Nkechi decided to seek counsel from a pastor after a Sunday service. But something dramatic happened before the end of the service. The Pastor, midway into the service, halted and said he wasn't going to continue with his message until he delivered a message he had for someone. Then he went on and on about how God speaks to people through the Holy Spirit but how they often ignore it because it runs contrary to their expectations. He urged the congregation to remember that "God's ways are not our ways." Nkechi broke down weeping under the weight of conviction. Still unsure about the voice in her head, Nkechi left the service with three questions on divorce. If she could have answers to them, she would reconsider her decision.

At the next Sunday service, the pastor paused again, mid-service, and proceeded to answer all the questions she had on divorce. That was all the confirmation she needed. She asked God for forgiveness, for doubting and met with a pastor to clarify her marital situation and what God was asking her to do. She confronted her sceptical parents and told them of God's instructions to her. A week later, she met her husband and told him she was coming back. Things had not changed, but she was willing to take a leap of faith with God. She drew strength from what the pastor had told her, "You are the light of the world. And you must bring light over your husband and your home." She would weep at night, but remain in prayer daily. She remained committed to church and to the department which she had joined.

The crossover night of that year, when she got back home, she met her excited husband who told her that year was his year of turnaround. Things began to take a turn for the better. She continued to pray for her husband and continued in the Word of God." God started to open her eyes to what marriage is all about, what the duty of the wife is, as prescribed in Ephesians 5:22-24:

'Wives, submit to your husbands as to The Lord. For the husband is the head of the wife as Christ is the head of the church, his body of which he is the saviour. Now as the church submits to Christ, so also wives should submit to their husband in everything.'

Nkechi was determined to hold on to God's Word in its entirety. She prayed and asked God to give her the Grace and strength to be submissive. The more submissive she was, the more he would misbehave. But she kept her sights on God despite the contrary opinions of her friends. "Why are you still there?" "Don't be stupid, leave him," they said. She would listen but say to herself, "they are talking from the flesh, but she was operating by the Holy Spirit."

Nkechi believes God opened her eyes to the meaning of true love when she yielded herself to Him in obedience and submitted to her husband.

Most people don't get what the meaning of love is. They limit it to romantic gestures such as buying of gifts and going on vacation to exotic locations. But love is much more. Love is patient, love is kind, it does not envy, it does not boast, it is not proud. It is not rude, it is not self-seeking, it is not easily angered, and it keeps no record of wrongs. Love does not delight in evil but rejoices with the truth. It always protects, always trusts, always hopes, always and preserves. (1 Corinthians 13:4-7).

Nkechi discovered its true meaning first hand, through fiery trials and temptations, and she came out on the other side victorious. Nkechi had applied the love of God, as prescribed above, to test her own love for her husband. Her husband became loving and caring. She had set an example of love and the results had been amazing. Every successful marriage is built on the Word of God, and it urges us to love. Love never fails. It will not fail you. Let us look at a few practical steps we can take to bring the love of God into application in our marriages.

2

Marriage is from God

It was Dr. David Hubbard that said:

"Nothing but a scrap of paper--that's what a marriage license is!' This kind of extravagant statement is a symptom of the spirit of our age. With increasing frequency, marriage is being put down, cast aside, and overturned. But wait a minute! Aren't scraps of paper important? Is it not one of the marks of civilized men that they protect themselves against their savagery by scraps of paper? Sure, a wedding license is a scrap of paper, but so in an employment contract, your paycheck, a twenty dollar bill, the deed to your home, and the Constitution of the United States."

Marriage is a holy covenant before God. Malachi 2:14 says, "You ask, "why?" It is because The Lord is acting as the witness between you and the wife of your youth, because you have broken faith with her, though she is your partner, the wife of your marriage covenant."

Marriage is a relationship between a man and a woman in which they become one flesh. God takes marriage very seriously. Jesus died for our sins, so we should be able to forgive each other's mistakes and be united as one. God created Adam and Eve and designated Adam to be the head of the house and Eve his helpmeet. Eve came out of Adam's rib. So you did not marry your spouse for the sake of marrying. It is God that joined you two together even before you were born. In Ephesians 5:24-25, Apostle Paul tells the wives to submit to their husbands and husbands to love their wives. "Now as the church submits to Christ, so also wives submit to their husbands in everything. Husbands, Love your wives, just as Christ loved the church and gave himself up for her."

Let me ask" what is easier? To die for someone or to cook a meal for someone? Yet Apostle Paul said that husbands are to love their wives so much that they are willing to die for her. You see it's a lot easier to submit without loving, than to love without submitting. That is why the lie of the devil is attacking marriages and so many have gone for divorce due to issues arising from the issue of submission. What Apostle Paul meant by to lay down your life and die, is dying daily to the self for the Lord so that you can do His will and not your own; to please God and not yourself. Likewise to lay down your life for your wife is to think of your spouse's needs rather than yourself and work together as one. John 15:13 - 14 says "Greater love has no one than this, that he lay down his life for his friends. You are my friend if you do what I command." The core of the Christian faith is love; beginning with God's love in sending Christ to die for our sins. Romans 5:8 says, "But God demonstrates his own love for us in this: While we were still sinners, Christ died for us."

Marriage is from God. This is one of the reason the devil attacks it. Couples often fight over small issues that escalate and lead to separation or divorce. This will not be our portion. It is not easy but it can be avoided if each party maintains fidelity to their role; husbands as head, loving to the point of death, and wives, as helpmates, submitting and supporting. To my marriage my husband and I argued a lot. Looking back now those fights had their roots in each of us wanting our way.

According to Lionel Whitston, broken marriages begin to mend and communication is reestablished when one of the partners is willing to make a breakthrough and say, "Lord, begin with me. I am the one who needs to change, to love more deeply and more wisely." Even if you think your spouse is 100% wrong, when you stand in the presence of Christ you will begin to see that you, too, have shortcomings. You will discern where you have failed to accept responsibility for the marital relationship, and you will be able to say, "God, change me." The Christian is committed to follow

Christ who went all the way in love, all the time. So, for a start, stop demanding that your partner change his ways. Let God start changing you.

If you do not have God in your marriage you will be opening doors for an unwanted guest -the devil.

Marriage can be likened to the Trinity; God the Father, Son and Holy Spirit. Thus as father and the son, are one substance and man and wife are one flesh. Similarly as the Father and the Son share one spirit, the man and wife are one spirit.

There is only one king in a marriage, and that's Jesus. Allow Him in and He will make your marriage awesome. The mistake most people make in their marriage is that when there are issues they believe they can solve it themselves instead of them letting God fight their battles. I realised this when I was having issues. I was battling them with my own strength, until I decided to hand over my problems to God and continue my life as if I had no problems at all. Since then the issues in my life have reduced. This helped me to be more patient, less talkative, and less aggressive. The devil really battled with me. He wanted my marriage to fail, but the good Lord intervened. I remember seeking His face like never before one morning after the Holy Spirit woke me up with a quiet voice saying, "But seek ye first the kingdom of God and His righteousness, and all these things shall be added unto you" (Matthew 6:33). I did not want to believe it because it is not what I wanted to hear. I decided to see my pastor and he encouraged me to keep on praying. I prayed and came to the conclusion that my marriage would not fail because my God is not a failure. It was not easy but it was a good fight. Whatever battles you have in your marriage, God will surely show up for you. You only need to understand why God created marriage and obey His word. His ways are never our ways so we must trust Him.

If you are married or planning to marry, you must continually assess your willingness to keep the commandments that make the two of you one? The goal in marriage should be more than friendship; it should be oneness. Genesis 2:24 says:

"Therefore a man shall leave his father and mother and be joined to his wife and they shall become one flesh".

The man and woman are joined together by taking responsibility for each other's welfare and by loving their spouse above all. The two become one flesh in the intimacy and commitment of sex that is reserved for marriage.

Strong marriages include all these aspects:

1. The man leaves his parents and in a public act exchanges the marital vows with the woman who becomes his wife

2. The man and woman are joined together by taking responsibility for each other's welfare and by loving the mate above all others.

3. The two become one flesh in the intimacy and commitment of sexual union that is reserved for marriage.

As you strive to achieve a godly marriage, God will give you grace and strength.

God gave marriage as a gift to Adam & Eve. They were created perfectly for each other. Look at Genesis 2:21 – 23:

"And the Lord God caused a deep sleep to fall on Adam, and he slept; and He took one of his ribs, and closed up the flesh in its place. Then the rib, which the Lord God had taken from man, He made into a woman, and He brought her to the man. And Adam said: "this is now bone of my bones and flesh of my flesh; she shall be called Woman, because she was taken out of Man.""

That's how God has created your own marriage; you are the flesh of your husband's flesh and the bone of his bone. If you walk with that mind-set in your marriage, you will surely be blessed.

No matter what you are going through you can still have a blessed marriage. It is just how you handle the situation. If you focus on Jesus, God can turn your situation around. You need to be selfless, able to forgive and have good communication if you want a blessed marriage. The most important thing is that Jesus must be the saviour and the Lord of your life. So from today receive the Lord Jesus as the foundation of your marriage. There is no perfect marriage, but there is a blessed marriage. Selfishness is the major reason why there are issues in marriages. Someone once said, "if you wish to be miserable, think about yourself; about what you want, what you like; what respect people ought to pay you; and then to you nothing will be pure. You will spoil everything you touch; you will make misery for yourself out of everything good; you will be as wretched as you choose." That is why there should not be any chance for selfishness in marriage but instead in every marriage there should be selflessness. Selflessness needs to be a priority in marriage. In Philippians 2:3 it says "Do nothing out of selfish ambition or vein conceit, but in humility consider others better than yourselves." I think this verse should be displayed in every home and we should always remind ourselves of this directive of Apostle Paul.

If this can be obeyed we would have heaven on earth. Also men should remember that women are the weaker sex and should be given extra honour. 1 Peter 3:7 says, "Husbands, in the same way be considerate as you live with your wives, and treat them with respect as the weaker partner and as heirs with you of the gracious gift of love, so that nothing will hinder your prayers." Some men do not understand this principle and so do not honour their wives as God commanded. They think they should be king, but they do not want to honour their wives as queen, seeing them as inferior beings. That is not God's view of women. They are not inferior to men or less in any way than men, just different and given a different role in life. There are three characteristics you can display in your marriage; maturity, immaturity and magnanimity.

1. Maturity - when you are mature, it means you are able to help your spouse without complaining and submit to him joyfully.. It takes time to reach maturity in ones marriage,

but when you get there you will definitely have a blessed marriage.

2. Magnanimity. This is about being generous in forgiving. Ephesians 5:17 says, "Therefore do not be unwise, but understand what the will of the Lord is." Magnanimity means seeking to understand your spouse's thoughts, feelings and needs. Apostle Paul said, "Live with your wife according to knowledge." Studying is not easy. It is hard work but it can be fulfilling, especially as you see the progress you can make from one stage to the next. The study of your spouse's needs and feelings is not easy especially when they conflict with your need. But the alternative to understanding is foolishness and who wants that? John 15:12 says, "This is my commandment, that ye Love one another, as I have loved you."

1 Peter 1:22 says, "Seeing ye have purified your souls in obeying the truth through the Spirit unto unfeigned love of the brethren, see that ye love one another with a pure heart fervently." That is the

proof of love. So you cannot say you love God and do not obey Him, you are only lying to yourselves. That is why Jesus said in Luke 6:46: "And why call ye me, Lord, Lord, and do not the things which I say?" To say you love God is to obey Him. God sees the two as synonymous, as one and the same. Only those who love God will submit their lives to Him and the authority of His word. Likewise if we love our spouses, we will submit to one another in the fear of The Lord. Marriages require both parties to be balanced and successful. It can't be only one person making an effort if both parties are able to follow God's blueprint, it will always produce a fruitful and blessed marriage.

Communication

A few years ago, the Harry S. Truman Library in Independence, MO made public 1,300 recently discovered letters that the late President wrote to his wife, Bess, over the course of a half-century. Mr. Truman had a lifelong rule of writing to his wife every day they were apart. He followed this rule whenever he was away on official business or whenever Bess left Washington to visit her beloved Independence. Scholars are examining the letters for any new light they may throw on political and diplomatic history. For our part, we were most impressed by the simple fact that every day he was away, the President of the United States took time out from his dealing with the world's most powerful leaders to sit down and write a letter to his wife.

If you want to be happy, healthy, successful, and live longer, give your spouse a kiss before you go to work each day. That's the conclusion of a study conducted by a group of German physicians and psychologists, in cooperation with insurance companies. According to Dr. Arthur Sazbo, the study found that those who kiss their spouse each morning miss less work because of illness than those who do not. They also have fewer auto accidents on the way to work. They earn 20 to 30 percent more monthly and they live about five years more than those who don't even give each other a peck on the cheek. The reason for this, says Dr. Sazbo, is that the kissers begin the day with a positive attitude. A kiss signifies a sort of seal of approval in the eyes of Dr. Sazbo and his colleagues and, they believe, those who don't experience it, for whatever reason, go out the door feeling not quite right about themselves. Whether you give this study any credence or not, an au revoir kiss every morning can do you no harm.

What the efficacy of the kiss and the example of Harry Truman's daily letters signify is that communication, in word and deed, is vital for a marriage to succeed. We should learn to communicate more with our spouses. Make them your best friend so that it will be easier for you to talk to each other on any issue. The secret of getting on well with your spouse is to apply the principle in Luke 6:31, which says "And as ye would that men should do to you, do ye also to them likewise." Communication means the act or process of using words, sounds, signs or behaviours to express or exchange information. Not all men like talking, some, for example, communicate better by sending texts. So study whatever means of communication works best for your husband, then try to use that means to communicate with him instead of forcing him to talk. This is very important in one's marriage and this is best when it can be achieved in the early years of the marriage.

Here is what Apostle Paul said in 1 Corinthians 1:10: "Now I beseech you, brethren, by the name of our Lord Jesus Christ, that ye all speak the same thing, and that there be no divisions among you; but that ye be perfectly joined together in the same mind and in the same judgement." Your marriage will become a happy mutually satisfactory one if both couples set their sights on unity, ministering to each other and communicating with each other in the proper Spirit. As Christians, you will find strength to do this as you pray and as you remember the exhortation in Ephesians 4:32: "And be ye kind one to another, tender-hearted, forgiving one another, even as God for Christ's sake hath forgiven you."

As you strive to achieve a godly marriage, God will give you strength and grace.

Before going any further, take a look at what the Bible says concerning marriage:

Gen 2:18 – 24	Marriage is God's idea
Gen. 24:58-60	Commitment is essential to a successful marriage
Songs of Songs 4:9-10	Romance is important
Jeremiah 33:10	Marriage holds times of great joy
Malachi 2:14-15	Marriage creates the best environment for raising children
Matthew 5:32	Unfaithfulness breaks the bond of trust, the foundation fall relationships
Matthew 19:6	Marriage is permanent
Romans 7:2-3	Ideally, only death should dissolve marriage
Ephesians 5:21-33	Marriage is based on principled practice of love, not feelings
Ephesians 5:23-32	Marriage is a living symbol of Christ and the church

Hebrews 13:4   Marriage is good and honourable

There is no need for marriages to fail – listen to God's word. God is very clear in the bible about the destruction of divorce, about the need to humbly consider the other person's needs above our own, about being truthful with each other and about avoiding sexual immorality. "I hate divorce, says The Lord God of Israel, and I hate a man's covering himself with violence as well as with garment," says The Lord Almighty. So guard yourself in your spirit, and do not break faith." This means we should have the same commitment to marriage that God has to his promises with His people. There must be passion in our marriage relationship to keep the commitment and sex satisfying, but this passion is only for our spouse.

Matthew 19:6 says "So they are no longer two but one. Therefore what God has joined together, let man not separate." Jesus' focus was on marriage rather than divorce. He pointed out that God intended marriage to be permanent.

Deuteronomy 24:1-4 says "If a man marries a woman who becomes displeasing to him because he finds something indecent about her, and he writes her a certificate of divorce, gives it to her and sends her out of his house, and after she leaves his house she becomes the wife of another man, and her second husband dislikes her and writes her a certificate of divorce, gives it to her and sends her from his house, or if he dies, then her first husband, who divorced her, is not allowed to marry her again after she has been defiled. That would be detestable in the eyes of the Lord. Do not bring sin upon the land the Lord your God is giving you as an inheritance."

This passage could seem like it is supporting divorce, but it is not. It is just recognizing a practise that already existed in Israel. Divorce was a permanent and final act for the couple. This restriction was to prevent casual remarriage after a separation. The intention was to make people think twice before divorcing.

God offers you a relationship with himself freely, just as marriage is a free choice. People have a choice to marry or not to marry. Matthew 19:10-12 says, "The disciples said to him, "if this is the situation between a husband and wife, it is better not to marry." Jesus replied, "Not everyone can accept this word, but only those to whom it has been given. For some are eunuchs because they were born that way; others were made that way by men; and others have renounced marriage because of the kingdom of heaven. The one who can accept this should accept it."

There are also many good reasons for not marrying, one being to have more time to work for God's kingdom. Don't assume that God wants everyone to marry. For many it may be better if they don't. Be sure that you are prayerfully seeking God's will before involving yourself in the lifelong commitment of marriage. Some have physical limitations that prevent their marrying, while others choose not to marry because in their particular situation they can serve God better as single people. Jesus was not teaching us to avoid marriage because it is inconvenient or takes away our freedom. That would be selfishness. A good reason to remain single is to use the time and freedom to serve God.

How God Sees Marriage?

From the beginning, marriage was not Adam's idea it was God's idea. It was God who gave him Eve as his wife.
Solomon says: "Houses and riches are an inheritance from fathers, but a prudent wife is from the Lord" (Proverbs 19:14).
We also see that marriage is good. Solomon says in another place:
"He who finds a wife finds a good thing, and obtains favour from the Lord" (Proverbs 18:22).

We also see how strong the marriage bond is, so strong that they are no longer two but are joined together as one flesh. So you did not simply get married, it is a favour from God and God chose your spouse for you. Remember the vows you took when you got married? For better or worse, for richer or poorer, till death do you part? These are very strong vows. Here is what Jesus said when He was asked about marriage:

"The Pharisees also came to Him, testing Him, and saying to Him, 'Is it lawful for a man to divorce his wife for just any reason?' And He answered and said to them, 'Have you not read that He who made them at the beginning "made them male and female," and said, "For this reason a man shall leave his father and mother and be joined to his wife, and the two shall become one flesh"? So then, they are no longer two but one flesh. Therefore what God has joined together, let not man separate.' They said to Him, 'Why then did Moses command to give a certificate of divorce, and to put her away?' He said to them, 'Moses, because of the hardness of your hearts, permitted you to divorce your wives, but from the beginning it was not so. And I say to you, whoever divorces his wife, except for sexual immorality, and marries another, commits adultery; and whoever marries her who is divorced commits adultery'" (Mat. 19:3-9).

In this passage in 1 Corinthians 11-12 we also see how dependent a man and a woman are on each other. They need each other. Paul says: "Nevertheless, neither is man independent of woman, nor woman independent of man, in the Lord.

For as the woman was from the man even so the man also is through the woman; but all things are from God" (1 Cor. 11:11, 12).

First, men and women should remain virgins until marriage. All sexual relations outside marriage are forbidden by God and are referred to as fornication. It is a sin, which is extremely damaging to those concerned, to society and to marriage as an institution. 1 Corinthians 6:18-20 " Flee from sexual immorality. All other sins a man commits are outside his body, but he who sins sexually sins against his own body. Do you not know that your body is a temple of the Holy Spirit, who is in you, whom you have received from God?

You are not your own; you were bought at a price. Therefore honour God with your body."

After marriage one is to have sexual relations only with their marriage partner. Sexual relations with any other is adultery, which also earned the death penalty under the Old Covenant. We read in Hebrews 13:4 that God wants marriage to be preserved from the damage caused by these two sins:

"Marriage is honourable among all, and the bed undefiled; but fornicators and adulterers God will judge" (Heb. 13:4).

From this text we see once more that marriage is pure and holy. Fornication and adultery damage marriage, and God will hold those who engage in such practices responsible on the Day of Judgment.

The marriage contract includes sexual responsibilities. Paul says:

"Let the husband render to his wife the affection due her, and likewise also the wife to her husband. The wife does not have authority over her own body, but the husband does. And likewise the husband does not have authority over his own body, but the wife does. Do not deprive one another except with consent for a time, that you may give yourselves to fasting and prayer; and come together again so that Satan does not tempt you because of your lack of self-control" (1 Cor. 7:3-5).

Sexual temptations are difficult to withstand because they appeal to the normal and natural desires that God has given us. Married couples have the responsibility to care for each other; so husband and wife should not neglect themselves, sexually from each other, but should fulfil each other's needs and desires.

The wife is to submit to the authority of her husband and the husband is to love his wife as his own body:

"Wives, submit to your own husbands, as to the Lord. For the husband is head of the wife, as also Christ is head of the church; and He is the Saviour of the body. Therefore, just as the church is subject to Christ, so let the wives be to their own husbands in everything. Husbands, love your wives, just as Christ also loved the church and gave Himself for it, that He might sanctify and cleanse it with the washing of water by the word, that He might present it to Himself a glorious church, not having spot or wrinkle or any such thing, but that it should be holy and without blemish. So husbands ought to love their own wives as their own bodies; he who loves his wife loves himself. For no one ever hated his own flesh, but nourishes and cherishes it, just as the Lord does the church. For we are members of His body, of His flesh and of His bones. 'For this reason a man shall leave his father and mother and be joined to his wife, and the two shall become one flesh.' This is a great mystery, but I speak concerning Christ and the church. Nevertheless let each one of you in particular so love his own wife as himself, and let the wife see that she respects her husband" (Eph. 5:22-33).

This does not mean that a man may misuse his authority, because if he loves his wife he will sacrifice for her as Christ did for the church. It does mean, however, that he is the head of the family. As the head he also bears the first responsibility. He can provide the needed leadership only if his wife respects and submits to his authority.

God's regulations in relation to marriage are strict. This is because He values marriage highly for the well-being of man. God's laws and regulations have no other purpose than the ultimate happiness of man. Let us trust the word of God in this matter. Marriage is His gift to us. He will help us to have good marriages if we obey His word and if we pray for His blessings, help and guidance.

3

Keeping a Healthy Marriage

It was John Graham that said, "Even if marriages are made in heaven, man has to be responsible for the maintenance." You can make your marriage beautiful. It all depends on you. People look for a perfect relationship but there is no such thing. It is what you put into your relationship that you will get out of it. You will need God's wisdom and understanding to have a great marriage.

Marriage is like any investment. You want to make profit from your investments, and so it is in marriage- you want your emotional and physical investment to be rewarded with a healthy, happy marriage. You need to study your husband's needs. Try to learn what he dislikes and likes, try to understand him then your marriage would be healthy.

We need to work hard on our marriages because that will please God.

Psalm 34:12-14 says, "Who is the man who desires life, and loves many days, that he may see good? Keep your tongue from evil, and your lips from speaking deceit. Depart from evil and do good; seek peace and pursue it."

There is a lot we can learn from this scripture. We can apply it in the following ways to keep our marriage healthy:

Control our tongues - We women love to talk. We are quick to talk but slow to listen so we should learn to be listeners. Often, we use our tongues to destroy, and by the time we have realised the effect of our tongues it might be too late. Let's start to be quiet and not be argumentative with our spouses. A woman seeking counsel from Dr. George W.

Crane, the psychologist, confided that she hated her husband, and intended to divorce him. "I want to hurt him all I can," she declared firmly. "Well, in that case," said Dr. Crane, "I advise you to start showering him with compliments. When you have become indispensable to him, when he thinks you love him devotedly, then start the divorce action. That is the way to hurt him." Some months later the wife returned to report that all was going well. She had followed the suggested course. "Good," said Dr. Crane. "Now's the time to file for divorce." "Divorce!" the woman said indignantly. "Never. I love my husband dearly!"

Avoid subjects that will cause disagreements. Give more compliments than complaints. Just because one keeps quiet does not mean that they are stupid. They are just preventing their marriage from being destroyed. We should learn to apologise to our husbands to maintain peace in our marriage.

I only learnt to control my tongue long after I was married. It was not easy but I was focusing on Jesus and I knew what I wanted to achieve in my marriage and I knew it would please God. I always remind myself that I am a helpmate, so it does not matter to me if I look stupid.

Do good to each other - no matter what your spouse does to you, do not react based on their actions. Sometimes we reward bad behaviour with equally bad or worse behaviour, but we should always do good no matter what, and God will definitely bless you. Treat each other well, no matter what the circumstances are because of your love for God.

When your husband does not treat you well and God is telling you to be good to him anyway, it is not easy at all, but with God's grace it is possible.

In my case, I kept my focus on Jesus and kept reminding myself that all I was doing was for God. Avoid satisfying your flesh and let the Holy Spirit take control. Let call on the Holy Spirit to help us continue to do what is right when we feel our husband is not treating us right. It is difficult but it can be achievable. Where is your focus, is it on man or God? Whatever you do, do it for God and not man then it will not bother you. God says do good so follow His commands and all will be well. All I do for my husband, I do joyfully with no complaints and God has been helping me and blessing me.

Seek peace and pursue it - In his classic work on the Beatitudes titled The Heavenly Octave, F.W. Boreham included this passage: "The ideal peacemaker is the man who prevents the peace from being broken. To prevent a battle is the best way of winning a battle. I once said to a Jewish rabbi, 'I have heard that at a Jewish wedding a glass is broken as part of the symbolism of the ceremony. Is that a fact?' 'Of course it is,' he replied. 'We hold aloft a glass, let it fall and be shattered to atoms, and then, pointing to its fragments, we exhort the young people to guard jealously the sacred relationship into which they have entered since, once it is fractured, it can never be restored.'"

A person that wants peace cannot be argumentative and contentious. Because peaceful relationships come from our efforts at peace making, work hard at living in peace with your spouse each day.

If you want a healthy marriage avoid arguments. In the heat of an argument you might say things that you would regret later on. Once you say something, you cannot take it back.

The most important thing in one's life besides a relationship with God is your spouse. You can have everything but if you lack good relationships, you will be unfulfilled and empty.

God wants you to enjoy your spouse; He divinely connected you with your husband. Here are some tips that will help make your marriage stronger:

- Work on being more patient with your spouse – understanding, compassionate.
- Do not go to bed angry – this will allow the devil to come into your marriage
- Lighten up – Proverbs 15:13 says, "A merry heart makes a cheerful countenance, but by sorrow of the heart the spirit is broken."

- Avoid touchy subjects when possible.

- Accept your spouse for who they are. Ephesians 4:29 says "Do not let any unwholesome talk come out of your mouth, but only what is helpful for building others up according to their needs, that it may benefit those who listen."

- Learn to forgive and let go – Ephesians 4:32 says "And be kind to one another, tender hearted, forgiving one another, even as God in Christ forgave." Jesus doesn't hold things against us when we sin.

- Recognise strife when it starts and stop before it gets out of hand – Proverbs 17:14 says "The beginning of strife is like releasing water; therefore stop contention before a quarrel starts."

- Be a peace maker – James 3:18 says "Now the fruit of righteousness is sown in peace by those who make peace." Proverbs 12:20 says, "Deceit is in the heart of those who devise evil, but counsellors of peace have joy." Proverbs 16:7 says, "When a man's ways please the Lord, He makes even his enemies to be at peace with him." Matthew 5:9 says, "Blessed is the peacemakers, for they shall be called sons of God." Ephesians 4: 2-3 says "With all lowliness and gentleness, with longsuffering, bearing with one another in love, endeavouring to keep the unity of the spirit in the bond of peace."

- Dress well for your husband - most people take their husband for granted. When you were not married you used to dress well to attract your husband but as soon as you got married all that stopped. You should continue to dress well for your husband.

Know that where there is peace, God gives a blessing so whenever you try to act out of love remember God's Word and ask the Holy Spirit to help you.

Things to work on in your relationship:
➢ Praying together
➢ Sharing feelings together
➢ Keep dating even after marriage

- ➤ Sexual agreement – agree on how many times a week you want to be having sex
- ➤ Budget your money
- ➤ Read the Bible together
- ➤ Get a mentor
- ➤ Set boundaries in how you both interact with members of the opposite sex
- ➤ Put limits on how much time you spend alone watching TV or using the computer

Enjoy the different seasons (God will hold your hands through the storm)

4

Keeping a Godly Marriage

The Christian's ultimate goal should not be to just have a "good" marriage but to be godly in your marriage. A godly marriage is one in which at least one person shows Christ in the marriage and keeps God's word in their relationship with their spouse. This does not just happen per chance bit you need to work at it.

1 Peter 3: 1 – 6 says "Wives, likewise, be submissive to your own husbands, that even if some do not obey the word, they, without a word, may be won by the conduct of their wives. When they observe your chaste conduct accompanied by fear. Do not let your adornment be merely

outward-arranging the hair, wearing gold, or putting on fine apparel rather let it be the hidden person of the heart, with the incorruptible beauty of a gentle and quiet spirit, which is very precious in the sight of God. For in this manner, in former times, the holy women who trusted in God also adorned themselves, being submissive to their own husbands, as Sarah obeyed Abraham, calling him lord, whose daughters you are if you do good and are not afraid with any terror."

Being a godly wife starts with the right priorities: You will need to have a good personal relationship with God – Matthew 6:33 says "But seek first the kingdom of God and His righteousness, and all these things shall be added to you."

When I was going through my challenges this is the word God gave me and since then I have been doing God's work. I joined a department at The Fountain of Life Church, hosted a home fellowship and started my ministry called "Virtuous Women" and God has been doing great things in my marriage. So if you seek God, God will do wonders in your life and marriage.

Ministering to your husband – Proverbs 18:22 says "He who finds a wife finds a good thing, and obtains favour from the Lord." Proverbs 19:14 says, "Houses and riches are an inheritance from fathers, but a prudent wife is from the Lord." Do what God has instructed you as a wife and your husband will call you blessed then you are the woman God has created to be a virtuous woman which should be the goal of every woman.

Looking after your children – 2 Timothy 1:5 says "When I call to remembrance the genuine faith that is in you, which dwelt first in your grandmother Lois and your mother Eunice, and I am persuaded is in you also."
Keeping your home – Titus 2:5 says, "To be discreet, chaste, home-makers, good, obedient to their own husbands, that the word of God may not be blasphemed."

Then adding whatever other activities, time and energy permits – Proverbs 31:10 says "Who can find a virtuous wife? For her worth is far above rubies." Proverbs 31:31: "Give her of the fruit of her hands, and let her own works praise her in the gates."

5

Investment in Marriage

In order to uncover the processes that destroy unions, marital researchers study couples over the course of years, and even decades, and retrace the star-crossed steps of those who have split up back to their wedding day. What they are discovering is unsettling. None of the factors one would guess might predict a couple's durability actually does: not how in love a newlywed couple say they are; how much affection they exchange; how much they fight or what they fight about. In fact, couples who will endure and those who won't look remarkably similar in the early days.

Yet when psychologists Cliff Notarius of Catholic University and Howard Markman of the University of Denver studied newlyweds over the first decade of marriage, they found a very subtle but telling difference at the beginning of the relationships. Among couples who would ultimately stay together, 5 out of every 100 comments made about each other were putdowns. Among couples who would later split, 10 of every 100 comments were insults. That gap magnified over the following decade, until couples heading downhill were flinging five times as many cruel and invalidating comments at each other as happy couples. "Hostile putdowns act as cancerous cells that, if unchecked, erode the relationship over time," says Notarius, who with Markman coauthored the new book We Can Work It Out. "In the end, relentless unremitting negativity takes control and the couple can't get through a week without major blowups."

All marriages, no matter how good they are, can be made better. There are some basic qualities a marriage has to have in order to be successful. Both of you need to be 100% committed to the relationship and willing to invest time and energy. Both husband and wife need to communicate effectively with each other, know how to resolve their differences, and learn to be flexible. A good relationship requires a lot of hard work. Marriage is a lifetime investment, and the seeds you sow will manifest into the marriage you eventually have. Remember you are both coming from two separate backgrounds and joining as one flesh. So as women, we need to adapt to our husband's ways for peace and a successful marriage.

Some people are married to unbelievers so it is the Christian spouse who should try to win the other to Christ. Marriage is permanent so you cannot decide that since my spouse is not a Christian you can divorce your spouse. No way.

It is not the will of God. Just continue praying for that spouse and by your actions they will be converted.

Right now, marriage is not operating as God had planned. This is why so many couples have marital problems and because of selfishness people are opting for divorce. God has clearly told us the approach to take. By wives being submissive to our husbands and by husbands loving their wives as Christ loves the church. Women are helpmates and men should be head. Ephesians 5:21-23 says "Submitting to one another in the fear of God. Wives submit to your own husbands, as to The Lord. For the husband is head of the wife, as also Christ is head of the church; and He is the saviour of the body."

When we ignore His counsel we rebel against God. Perhaps if we were more attentive to the instructions of our creator we would find that marriage works much better. The best marriage is the marriage that is built on the foundation of God's word. Most women find it difficult to submit to their husband, not realising that that is one of the keys to a successful marriage. When you submit to your spouse it is actually easier to get what you want from him.

Marriage Should Be About Giving

A couple married for 15 years began having more than usual disagreements. They wanted to make their marriage work and agreed on an idea the wife had. For one month they planned to drop a slip in a "Fault" box. The boxes would provide a place to let the other know about daily irritations. The wife was diligent in her efforts and approach: "leaving the jelly top off the jar," "wet towels on the shower floor," "dirty socks not in hamper," on and on until the end of the month. After dinner, at the end of the month, they exchanged boxes. The husband reflected on what he had done wrong. Then the wife opened her box and began reading. They were all the same, the message on each slip was, "I love you!"

We tend to focus on the wrong things. We expect our husband's to do so much for us, and when they do not do all that we want, we get upset. The biblical teaching about marriage urges us to put our spouses first. We need to seek to understand what God is driving at. Marriage is not about women serving men. It is about men and women serving each other. If we focus on what the other person is supposed to do for us we have missed Paul's point. Ephesians 5:21 says, "Submit to one another out reverence for Christ." The content of this command is one of MUTUAL submission. The focus is on giving not getting; contrary to public view, the biblical view of marriage is not one sided. It is not about women becoming servants of men... it is about two people working hard to give of themselves, to enrich and encourage each other. In 1 Peter 3:1 it says "Wives, in the same way be submissive to your husband so that, if any of them do not believe the word, they maybe won over without words by the behaviour of their wives."

➤ In 1 Peter 2, Paul tells us to submit to authorities and show respect for everyone. As Jesus Christ sacrificed His life he says, "wives in the same way" and husbands in the same way". Jesus did not live for what He could get from others. He gave His life so that we might know life. We live at a time when the primary focus is on what we are getting from the relationship. The biblical teaching about marriage urges us to put each other first. Our concern should be what we can give to the relationship. This is the same for both men and women. I've noticed that many women complain that their husband's do not help out. I say, why worry about it? Why don't you just ask the Holy Spirit to give you the strength to do all you need to do? Instead of complaining, why not find a way to make your relationship stronger? Your complaints should be more like: I am having trouble finding more ways to demonstrate my love

- I am struggling looking for a way to be more encouraging to my spouse. They have such talent and it would be a shame for them not to use it.
- I am frustrated that I do not do more for my spouse.
- I wish I could love my spouse more completely.

Keep in mind as you weather those martial storms, that we're warned in 1 Corinthians 7:2728: "Are you married? Do not seek a divorce. Are you unmarried? Do not look for a wife. But if you do marry, you have not sinned; and if a virgin marries, she has not sinned. But those who marry will face many troubles in this life, and I want to spare you this."

Colossians 3: 18-19 says "Wives, submit to your husbands, as is fitting in the Lord. Husbands, love your wives and do not be harsh with them." 1 Peter 3:7 says "Husbands, in the same way be considerate as you live with your wives, and treat them with respect as the weaker partner and as heirs with you of the gracious gift of life, so that nothing will hinder your prayers."

People get married based on their own feelings and do things by what they feel. It is wrong. We should focus on God and obey His directives.

1 Corinthians 7: 17- 40 "Nevertheless, each person should live as a believer in whatever situation the Lord has assigned to them, just as God has called them. This is the rule I lay down in all the churches. Was a man already circumcised when he

was called? He should not become uncircumcised. Was a man uncircumcised when he was called? He should not be circumcised. Circumcision is nothing and uncircumcision is nothing. Keeping God's commands is what counts. Each person should remain in the situation they were in when God called them.

Were you a slave when you were called? Don't let it trouble you—although if you can gain your freedom, do so. For the one who was a slave when called to faith in the Lord is the Lord's freed person; similarly, the one who was free when called is Christ's slave. You were bought at a price; do not become slaves of human beings. Brothers and sisters, each person, has a responsibility to God and should remain in the situation they were in when God called them.

6

Keeping your Christian Marriage Strong and Healthy

Pray Together - The Lord says that if two gather together in prayer, He is in the midst of them. So praying with your spouse helps to keep God in your marriage. It also brings you closer to each other. Pray for your marriage and also for each other.

Respect and Honour each other - commit to making important decisions together. This is one of the best ways to develop trust as a couple.

Encourage each other to grow together - Hebrews 10:24-25 says " And let us consider how we may spur one another on toward love and good deeds. Let us not give up meeting together as some are in the habit of doing, but let us encourage one another - and all the more as you see the Day approaching."

Read the Bible together as much as possible.

Be swift to hear and slow to speak. It is important that we are good listeners and patient. Our responses should be considered and anger should be managed. James 1:19-20 says "My dear brothers, take note of this: Everyone should be quick to listen, slow to speak and slow to get angry, for man's anger does not bring about the righteous life that God desires.

Make time to communicate with each other. Protect and Honour your marriage vows.

Do not let others come between your marriages - Set aside special, regular times to continue developing your romance. It is vital to maintain a secure and intimate marriage. Your job, children and hobbies should not come between you and your spouse. Although children are really a blessing from God, it should not come to a point where they come in between the two of you. They are given as a blessing to bind you closer and not to drive you both apart.

Look for creative ways to say how much you love each other. Here are 21 great inexpensive ways to tell the love of your life just how much you care.

1. Make a homemade card with a picture of the two of you on the cover. Get ideas for a verse by spending a few minutes browsing through a card shop.

2. Write a poem. It doesn't have to rhyme.

3. Send a love letter listing the reasons "Why I love you so much."

4. Pledge your love for a lifetime. Write it on calligraphy or design it on a desktop computer and print it out on parchment paper and have it framed.

5. Plan a surprise lunch, complete with picnic basket, sparkling grape juice and goblets.

6. Bake a giant cookie and write "I love you" with heart shaped redhots or frosting. (Don't worry about the calories, it's not for eating!)
7. Make a coupon book and include coupons for a back rub, a compromise when about to lose an argument, a listening ear when needed, and doing the dishes when the other cooks.
8. Kidnap the car for a thorough washing and detailing.
9. Design your personal crest combining symbols that are meaningful to both of you.
10. Compose a love song.
11. Arrange for someone to sing a favorite love song to you and your love when you're together.
12. Call a radio station and have them announce a love message from you and make sure your love is listening at the right time.
13. Make a big sign such as: "I Love You, Kristi. Love, Joe" and put it in front of your house or her apartment complex for the world to see.
14. Buy favorite fruits that aren't in season, like a basket of strawberries or blueberries.

15. Hide little love notes in the car, a coat pocket, or desk.

16. Place a love message in the "personal" section of the classified ads in your local paper.

17. Florist flowers aren't the only way to say "I love you." Pluck a single flower and write a message about how its beauty reminds you of your love. For greater impact, have it delivered at work.

18. Prepare a surprise candle light gourmet low-calorie dinner for two.

19. Write the story of the growth of your relationship from your perspective, sharing your emotions and your joys. What a treasure!

20. Make a paperweight from a smooth stone, paint it, and write a special love message on it.

21. Promise to change a habit that your love has been wanting you to change.

Thank God everyday for your husband/ wife and the life you have together - Be thankful.

Whatever you do you must put your husband first and make him happy by following his instructions. Even if you disagree with him just obey. If you disobey your husband you are disobeying The Almighty God. God says your husband is the head of the family and you are his helpmate. When he cannot meet his obligations and if you are able to, help him out. You are one. It will benefit both of you and your marriage will be stronger and more united. Another issue that usually comes up in marriage comes in the guise of the familiar notion that you marry the whole family. This is not scriptural. The Bible in Genesis 2:24 says, "Therefore a man shall leave his father and mother and be joined to his wife and they shall become one. You should not allow your extended family have too much influence in your marriage. Try solving your differences with each other. Put all your problems to God, the creator of Heaven and Earth, and the one who created marriage for our good.

I just want to emphasize that divorce is not an option at all. It should not come across one's mind because God hates divorce. 1 Corinthians 7:10-11 says "To the married I give this command (not I, but the Lord): A wife must not separate from her husband. But if she does, she must remain unmarried or else be reconciled to her husband. And a husband must not divorce his wife." Marriage is a good thing. Yes there will be bad times, but you can still be happy as long as you focus on God's word. Marriage is all about selflessness. If we could remove selflessness in our marriages then we would not have any issues. Try to understand your husband, communicate, do not keep strife and be submissive. If you have a good Christian character you can influence your husband if he is not a believer. This will only happen if you do things to please God and God will fight your battles for you. Try to have a forgiving heart so that your prayers will be answered and your blessing can be received. Have faith in God so you have something to hold onto when there are storms. Finally spend less time trying to change your husband- instead spend more time praying for your husband and work on yourself to be more Christ-like and everything else will be settled.

Finally, I cannot overemphasize the power of prayer to help heal your marriage. Below is a prayer you can say to help bring restoration to your troubled marriage:

Dear Lord,

I thank you for my husband. I thank you for being the centre of my marriage. Help me to love my spouse. Help me to be patient and kind, to bear all things, to believe all things, to hope for all things and endure all things. Give me the Grace to be a helpmate to my spouse as God has commanded me and to

become a virtuous woman so my
husband can call me blessed. My
spouse will be favoured. He shall be
the head and not the tail. And what
God has joined together no man will
put asunder, in Jesus' Name. Amen.

I hope you and your marriage are blessed by this
book.

Daily Prayer Points
For The Man You Love

"Her husband has full confidence in her and lacks nothing of value. She does him good, not harm, all the days of her life." (Proverbs 31:11 - 12)

It is very important to be a blessing to your husband and you can be one by praying for him. Here are practical prayer points you can apply in this regard:

Day 1

Pray that your husband will grow in grace and in the knowledge of Our Lord and Savior Jesus Christ. (2 Peter 3:18).

Pray that the Lord will guard his heart, grant him grace to meditate on the Word and that he will not be taken in by sin. (Prov. 4:23)

Day 2

Pray that your husband will fear The Lord and shun evil. (Prov. 3:7).

Ask the Lord to grant him the spirit of wisdom, knowledge and understanding.(Prov.9:10).

Day 3

Pray that your husband's sins should be washed away and that he should be cleansed (Ps. 51:2-4). Pray for your husband to act justly and to love mercy and to walk humbly before the Lord (Micah 6:8)

Day 4

Pray that your husband will love and care for you as his own body; and that God will grant him the grace to protect and provide (Eph. 5:25-29). Pray for your husband to love you and not be harsh with you (Col. 3:19).

Day 5

Pray that your husband will be faithful to his wedding vows (Prov. 20:6). Pray that your husband is made perfect for you and that he would be a good head over his family (Gen. 2:24)

Day 6

Pray that your husband will run when he sees danger (Prov.27:12). Pray for protection from every form of evil over your husband (John 17:15). Pray that he will not to fall into temptation and will be equipped to bear up under any that God allows (1 Corinthians 10:12-13).

Day 7

Pray that God will keep your husband from immoral women and protect his heart from illicit relationships with other women (Prov. 6:23-24 & 26).

Pray that your husband will not be in any situation that will open the door to him gratifying any sinful desire (Rom. 13:14)

Day 8

Pray that your husband will not lack anything and that he will take his spirituality seriously, serving the Lord (Rom. 12:11).

Pray that nothing your husband does will be in vain and pray against any discouragement (1 Corinthians 15:58).

Day 9

Pray that your husband will have wisdom on how to manage his finance (Prov. 23:4-5).

Pray that your husband will be a giver to those in need (Rom. 12:13).

Pray that your husband will not have the love of money and that he will be content with what he has, because God will never leave him nor forsake him (Hebrew. 13:5).

Day 10

Pray that your husband will follow the Word of God so that God can bless him (Prov. 20:7). Pray that whatever he does will be done in love, good conscience and a sincere faith (1Tim. 1:5).

Pray that your husband will not be disgraced at his workplace or in business and amongst outsiders (1 Tim. 3:7).

Pray for your husband to be strong in the Lord and in His mighty power so that he contend effectively with the devil.

Also pray that your husband should put on the full armor of God so when the day of trouble comes he will be able to stand firm (Eph. 6:10-12).

Day 11

Pray that your husband will do the will of God from his heart (Eph. 6:6). Pray that the fear of the Lord teaches your husband wisdom and humility (Prov. 15:33).

Day 12

Pray for faithfulness in your marriage, pray that your husband will enjoy you (Prov. 5:15).
Pray that your husband will not find you boring and he would find pleasure in you (Prov. 5:18). Pray that your husband will fulfill his marital duty to you and the family (1 Corinthians 7:3). Pray that there should be more love and freedom between the two of you (Song of Solomon 7:10).

Day 13

Pray that your husband will not indulge in any sinful nature rather you will serve one another in love (Gal. 5:13). Pray that God should remove any selfish ambition that your husband acquires and replace it with humility (Phil. 2:3-4).

Day 14

Pray that your husband will only utter good words that will lift your family up (Prov. 18:21).
Pray that the Holy Spirit helps your husband to control anger, bitterness and bad attitude towards others (Eph. 4:29).

Day 15

Pray that God will give your husband good and wise friends that will lift him up.
Pray that your husband will have friends who would help each other to become sharper (Prov. 27:17).

Day 16

Pray that your husband will remain healthy (1 Cor. 6:12).
Pray that whatever your husband does will glorify God (1 Corinthians 10:31).

Pray that any struggle your husband is going through will result in him being edified and God being glorified (2 Tim. 2:4).

Day 17

Pray that God will strengthen your husband, out of His glorious riches, with power through his Spirit in your husband's inner being (Eph. 3:16).
Pray that your husband will be more like Christ (1 Peter 2:21).
Pray that God will grant your husband the grace to keep studying the Bible and walking by its precepts. (1 Cor. 10:11).

Day 18

Pray that your husband will seek the kingdom of God first and not the things of the world (Matt. 6:33).
Pray that your husband will love God with all his heart, with all his soul and all his strength (Deut. 6:5).

Pray that your husband will make the most of every opportunity, because the days are evil (Eph. 5:16).

Pray for what you want to see happen in your husband's life and that God will reveal the steps he needs to take to accomplish them (Ps. 90:12).

Day 19

Pray that your husband will make efforts to do what will led to peace and to mutual edification (Rom. 14:19).

Pray for your husband to turn away from evil and do good, also to seek peace and pursue it (Ps. 34:14).

Day 20

Pray that your husband will continue to have the mind of Christ (Prov. 27:12).

Pray that your husband's thoughts will be subject to the control of the Lord (2 Cor. 10:5)

Day 21

Pray that your husband will not grieve for the joy of The Lord is his strength (Neh. 8:10).

Pray that your husband will be cheerful (Prov. 17:22).

Pray that God will fill your husband with joy in God's presence with eternal pleasures (Ps. 16:11).

Day 22

Pray that your husband will be kind and compassionate to others and be able to forgive those who wrong him. (Eph. 4:32).

Day 23

Pray that God will grant your husband the wisdom to train up your children in the way of the Lord (Eph. 6:4).

Pray that your husband will discipline your children in love (Col. 3:21).

Pray that your husband will be strong in the grace that is in Christ Jesus and be equipped to have faith in whatever he does (2 Tim. 2:1-2).

Day 24

Pray that your husband will grow in wisdom and stature, and in favor with God and men (Luke 2:52).

Pray that your husband will have good understanding and he will be faithful (Prov. 13:15).

Day 25

Pray that your husband will take heart and be strong in the hope that is in the Lord (Ps. 31:24). Pray that your husband will put on the full armor of God so that when the day of trouble comes he will be able to stand his ground (Eph. 6:13).

Day 26

God says he has a plan for your husband a plan to prosper and not to harm him, plans to give your husband hope and a future. Decree that this will be a reality in your husband's life in Jesus' name (Jer. 29:11).

Day 27

Pray that your husband will joyfully give himself as a living sacrifice for God's service (Rom. 12:1-2).

Pray that your husband will honor God with his body (1 Cor. 6:19-20).

Pray that your husband will practice what he preaches (1 Corinthians 9:27).

Day 28

Pray that your husband will be prayerful and spend more time with God in his spare time (1 Thess. 5:17).

Day 29

Pray that God will grant your husband the grace to make the most of every opportunity (Eph. 5:15-16).
Pray that your husband will manifest the fruit of the Spirit.(1 Cor. 12: 7).

Day 30

Pray that whatever your husband does he should work hard on it with all his heart, as working for God and not for men (Col. 3:23-24).

Day 31

Pray that your husband will be able to carry on the work of Jesus Christ and flee from evil (John 8:44)